MW01154269

Soaring Through
Glenn Curtiss's
Growth Mindset

Dream Big, Work Hard, Fly High

Written by
Jenna Tremaine

Illustrated by
Bonnie Lemaire

alo
PUBLISHING
INTERNATIONAL

Halo Publishing International
8000 W Interstate 10, #600
San Antonio, Texas 78230

First Edition, October 2022
Printed in the United States of America
ISBN: 978-1-63765-312-8
Library of Congress Control Number: 2022916810

Halo Publishing International is a self-publishing company that publishes adult fiction and non-fiction, children's literature, self-help, spiritual, and faith-based books. Do you have a book idea you would like us to consider publishing? Please visit www.halopublishing.com for more information.

How Glenn Curtiss is remembered today:

The Glenn H. Curtiss Museum located in Hammondsport, New York, is an educational institution that showcases the lifetime accomplishments of Glenn Curtiss.

Thank you to the Glenn Curtiss Elementary School:

Thank you to the students and staff at the Glenn Curtiss Elementary School in Hammondsport, New York. The elementary school is proud of being named after Glenn Curtiss. All the students and staff at the Curtiss school are living examples of the power of what it means to have a Growth Mindset. "Dream Big, Work Hard, Fly High" is a school motto that reflects the commitment of all students and staff to set goals, work hard, acknowledge feedback, and learn from mistakes. Through the use of this book, the history and accomplishments of Glenn Curtiss are celebrated and are utilized to spread this message about the pride in operating as a collaborative community also known as a family.

Thank you to the Glenn Curtiss Elementary School Principal, Mr. Joe Koehler, for assisting author Jenna Tremaine in emphasizing the message of Growth Mindset that this book encompasses.

Thank you to historian:

A huge thank-you to Rick Lisenrang, curator at the Glenn H. Curtiss Museum, for his help educating author Tremaine on the historical aspects that this book covers.

Many years ago in 1878, Glenn Hammond Curtiss was born in Hammondsport, New York. Glenn lived with his grandmother, who cared for him and was an inspiration in Glenn's work ethic. At a young age, Glenn dreamed big. His Grandmother often reminded him, "Glenn, if you work hard, you can always achieve your goals!"

When Glenn's family moved from the small village of Hammondsport to the big city of Rochester, he quickly gained a new hobby.

"Look, my very first bicycle!"

The bike was broken, but Glenn felt excited because he had a tinkering ability; he loved to take apart and fix things. Glenn always wondered, "How does this work? And where does that part go?" Glenn saw this as an opportunity.

Glenn spent a lot of time fixing bikes to make them work. He used a bicycle in his work as a messenger, so he spent a lot of time fixing that bike. He always felt great excitement when riding it.

Glenn thought, "What's next?"

He soon began to compete in bike races. Glenn was amazed! He could not believe the feeling that going fast gave him.

Glenn Curtiss was always dreaming bigger, and he was excited about finding new ways of going faster. He began experimenting and working with others, and one day Glenn had a wonderful idea!

"What if I put an engine on a bike? It would go faster than a regular bike!"

As always, Glenn worked hard at fixing and creating machines, not just for himself, but also to help those around him. His ideas and determination allowed him to start building powered bicycles.

As time passed, Glenn realized his growing passion for engines, and he focused on building and fixing engines for motorcycles. Of course, Glenn's need for speed had inspired him to begin racing these machines.

"Wow, he is so fast!"

"Who is that?"

"What is his name?"

People began to ask about Glenn. Many grew interested in not only Glenn's engines, but also his racing!

It was true that Glenn was competitive; this was what made him work so hard. In his races, Glenn often finished in second or third place. He did not always win, but he did not let that stop him.

Glenn felt encouraged to keep fixing and changing his engines so that he could do his best.

"I know what I need to do to reach success. I must work hard, not give up, and, most importantly, keep dreaming big."

Glenn's mindset set him up for success.

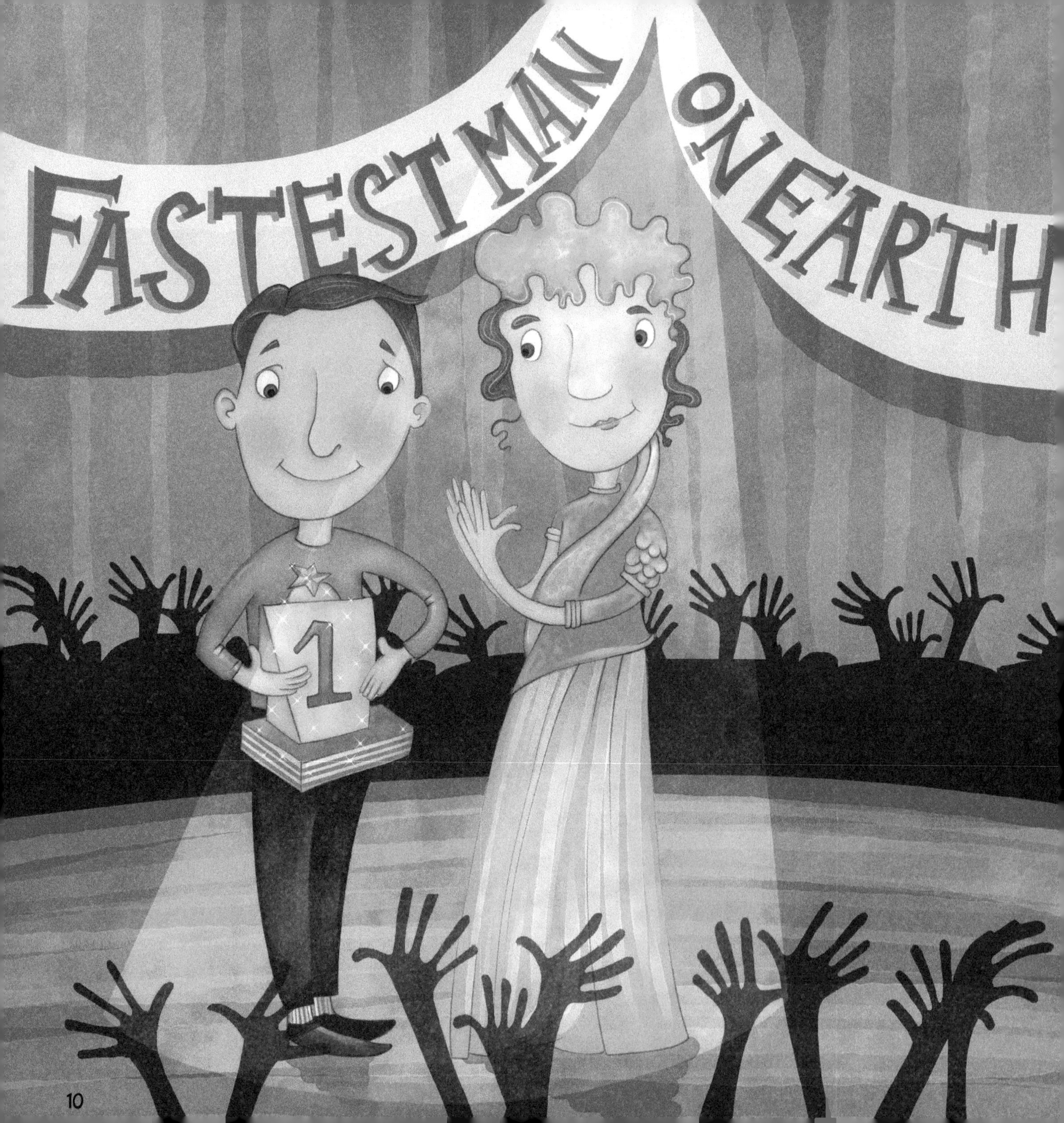
FASTEST MAN ON EARTH
1

After Glenn's hard work and the changes he made to his engines, he kept racing and became the fastest! Glenn felt happy; all his hard work showed, and he started winning.

Thanks to the speed that his great engines gave him, Glenn grew popular, and so did his engines. He soon became known as the Fastest Man on Earth.

Glenn always remembered his grandmother's encouraging words when he was a young boy. "If you work hard, you can always achieve your goals and learn from your mistakes."

Glenn felt lucky that his best friend, Lena, was always there to support his large dreams.

"You can do anything you put your mind to, Glenn!" often said Lena.

Those around Glenn encouraged him to keep dreaming big.

A special thing about Glenn was how he worked alongside others. As he grew popular, he attracted a large group of people who also created engines. Glenn was always willing to help them achieve their goals.

As Glenn continued to meet new people who inspired him, his dreams grew bigger.

Soon, Glenn would meet someone whom he would inspire and be inspired by. His name was Alexander Graham Bell.

"Wow, Alexander, it seems like you have some really great ideas. Let's work together!"

Alexander had ordered an engine from Glenn, and after meeting him, Alexander gave Glenn a warm invitation to join him in his aviation experiments.

Glenn did not have experience in aviation, but he felt excited, as it was something new that he could learn!

As Glenn worked with Alexander, he met pioneer aviators who inspired him. His curious mindset allowed him to watch, listen, and read all about planes, and what they needed to successfully fly. He knew that if he worked hard, he could achieve his goals and help others achieve theirs.

Glenn wanted to continue learning more about aviation. He was part of the Aerial Experiment Association (AEA) team. They worked hard together!

Glenn often asked his team questions that would help him learn and understand more. He was always seeking advice from others.

He began working on old projects and starting new projects with his AEA team. Glenn used what he knew about engines to help him develop new skills that would help design planes.

During his early life as an aviation pioneer, Glenn helped his AEA team reach their aviation goals before he achieved his own. Their first project was the Red Wing.

Glenn felt inspired by Thomas Selfridge, who had designed the Red Wing.

"This plane will be great!"

Glenn was always encouraging his team. His positivity made them feel and do their very best!

Soon, the Red Wing plane was ready for takeoff. Glenn helped his team prepare the plane for its flight on the ice of Keuka Lake.

As Glenn continued to help his team reach their goals, he could not stop dreaming about his own.

As time went on, Glenn learned, worked, and kept dreaming.

Next, it was time for Glenn's partner, Casey Baldwin, to work on his aviation project. The plane was called the White Wing, and Glenn noticed the different wings on the plane. He thought, "Great thinking, Casey, this will help the plane fly better!"

It was that time again. The team put their hard work to the test and officially flew the White Wing near Hammondsport.

Glenn felt excited for his team, but he kept dreaming big.

18

It was finally Glenn's turn! He would start working on the plane that he had been dreaming of. He knew that to achieve this goal, he must work hard.

So, Glenn began creating and designing his plane. But, of course, he did not work alone; he had the help of his team.

Glenn and his team worked hard to put all his ideas together. But this time, the project was different.

Throughout Glenn's life, he had always been on a quest to gain new skills so that he could do his very best. He had developed a Growth Mindset. This is what made Glenn's project so special.

Glenn's team began working hard to help him achieve his goals and design the plane. After a lot of hard work and long hours, Glenn's plane was named the June Bug.

Time passed, but the June Bug was just not ready yet. Glenn focused on what he could do to make the plane his very best!

"Thanks for all your hard work. I would never have been able to do this without my team!"

Of course, building the June Bug took time and was not easy. But Glenn's Growth Mindset allowed him to be a team leader, and that also made the project special.

Soon it was time for Glenn Curtiss to fly the June Bug.

"You got this, Glenn!"

"You worked so hard!"

"I can't wait to see the June Bug fly."

Glenn had so much support from those who inspired him.

THE FIRST FLIGHT SCHOOL

A E A
First flight

DREAM BIG

WORK HARD

FLY HIGH

That day was here! On June 4, 1908, Glenn took off in the June Bug for his flight near Hammondsport.

Because of Glenn's Big Dreams and his Hard Work, he was able to Fly High. He reached his goal to fly the June Bug, and he won the Scientific American trophy due to the successful flight. This was the first-ever flight award given.

After the flight, Glenn had a huge smile! He realized that he couldn't have achieved his goals, without his Growth Mindset.

The amazing feeling that flying gave Glenn inspired him to keep designing, building, and flying planes.

As time passed, Glenn continued working hard and became very popular in aviation. He focused on his new goals and designs, but, more importantly, he helped others achieve their own.

Glenn knew that aviation was something that could benefit those around him. He was inspired by so many; he wanted to keep inspiring others. So, he opened his own flight school to teach others how to fly.

Glenn's Growth Mindset continued to inspire those around him with the message—Dream Big, Work Hard, and Fly High!

Children's glossary

Growth Mindset: Working and never giving up. This mindset fosters the drive to learn, grow, and work with others while achieving your goals despite any challenges.

Aviation: Developing, designing, and flying airplanes.

Aircraft: A machine that flies through the air.

Pioneer: A person who develops or helps develop something new.

Printed in the USA
CPSIA information can be obtained
at www.ICGtesting.com
LVHW070614140823
755121LV00003B/55